CORNE VANDER

AMERICAN ENTREPRENEUR

DENNIS FERTIG

Boston, Massachusetts
Chandler, Arizona
Glenview, Illinois
Upper Saddle River, New Jersey

Illustrations

Operer, 1, 2, 3, 4, 5, 12, 15 Tim Jones; 8 Joe LeMonnier.

Photographs

Every effort has been made to secure permission and provide appropriate credit for photographic material.
The publisher deeply regrets any omission and pledges to correct errors called to its attention in subsequent editions.

Unless otherwise acknowledged, all photographs are the property of Pearson Education, Inc.

Photo locators denoted as follows: Top (T), Center (C), Bottom (B), Left (L), Right (R), Background (Bkgd)

6 Prints & Photographs Division, LC-USZC2-3436/Library of Congress; 7 Prints & Photographs Division, LC-DIG-pga-03828/Library of Congress; 9 Daguerreotypes Collection, Prints & Photographs Division, LC-USZC4-4160/Library of Congress; 10 FSA/OWI Collection, Prints & Photographs Division, LC-USF33- 012696-M4/Library of Congress; 11 Daguerreotypes Collection, Prints & Photographs Division, LC-USZC4-7421/Library of Congress; 13 Prints & Photographs Division, LC-USZC2-2531/Library of Congress; 14 Stereograph Cards Collection, Prints & Photographs Division, LC-DIG-stereo-1s01729/Library of Congress.

ISBN-13: 978-0-328-67637-8
ISBN-10:   0-328-67637-3

11   17

American Builder of Wealth

Cornelius Vanderbilt was a successful man who moved far from his beginnings as the son of a farmer. Starting with a $100 loan, this **entrepreneur** built new forms of transportation. He turned that loan into a huge transportation empire.

Vanderbilt was known as a tough and honest businessman. By the end of his life, he was also considered the richest man in the United States. His goal was to build power and wealth for himself and his family, but the country benefited as well. The web of steamship and railroad routes he created around the country transformed America, helping it grow larger and richer.

A Young Businessman

Vanderbilt was born in 1794 on Staten Island, New York, across a bay from Manhattan Island. Today Staten Island is part of New York City, but it was not then. In 1794, Staten Island was a quiet place of small villages and farms whose owners sold their products across the bay in the city.

Vanderbilt's father was one of those farmers who used his own boat to ferry goods across the water. Vanderbilt's mother grew some goods and sewed some of the other goods the family sold. She also managed the family's money and made loans. Acting much like a bank, she hoped to make a **profit** when people paid her back.

Cornelius Vanderbilt first used a ferry that had sails.

As a boy, Vanderbilt was independent and knew how to work hard. By age 11, he'd already sailed a ferry across the rough waters to Manhattan. He'd also quit school. School or no school, however, Vanderbilt kept on learning.

Young Vanderbilt was bigger and stronger than most other children his age. As a teenager, he already was bigger than most men. Vanderbilt did not hesitate to use his size, strength, and fists to settle disagreements.

Vanderbilt got his first lessons about money from his mother. When he was 16, she lent him $100 to buy his own boat and start his own ferry business. She hoped this would be enough to keep Vanderbilt from becoming a sailor and leaving home. She had no idea that her loan would help create the richest man in America.

The busy harbor of New York City

4

Soon, Vanderbilt's ferries were carrying farm produce to Manhattan. There were other ferry companies around, but Vanderbilt was a tireless and tough **competitor**. Vanderbilt always found ways to make his business more successful. At times that led to fights with other ferryboat owners.

As Vanderbilt earned more money from his ferry company, he began to **invest** in other companies as well. That meant he became part owner of them, and when they earned profits, he did as well.

When the United States fought Great Britain in the War of 1812, New York City was suddenly filled with troops. The military considered Vanderbilt tough, hard-working, and honest. They hired him and his ferries to carry soldiers and supplies all over New York City.

One of Vanderbilt's steamboats

A New Kind of Boat

In 1818, Vanderbilt sold his ferry business. Why would he sell something so successful? Vanderbilt has his eye on a new **technology**—steamboats. Vanderbilt went to work for Thomas Gibbons, who used the new ships powered by steam.

Vanderbilt was confident that steamboats would soon replace sailboats as the best water transportation. He wanted to learn as much as he could about them. He also gained another kind of experience. Gibbons's company was in a court battle with another ferry company. It had a **monopoly** on the steamboat business in New York. The state government allowed it to control all the ferry business on New York's harbors and rivers. Gibbons and Vanderbilt did not believe that this was fair. Ultimately Gibbons won the fight in the courts, but it took a long time.

Vanderbilt's First Steamship Company

Gibbons paid Vanderbilt well, and Vanderbilt saved well. In 1829, Vanderbilt had enough money to start his own company. The company used steamboats and stagecoaches to move people and goods between New York City and Philadelphia. Another company did the same thing. However, Vanderbilt found ways to make his costs and prices lower. When the other company's managers tried to cut its prices, Vanderbilt always outsmarted them. Vanderbilt was able to cut costs further and make sure that customers remained happy with his service.

In the end, the other company decided it couldn't compete against Vanderbilt, so it offered to buy his company instead. Vanderbilt agreed. With the money from that sale, Vanderbilt started a new steamboat company. This business operated on the Hudson River in New York.

Vanderbilt's steamboats traveled up and down the Hudson River.

By now, Vanderbilt was well known as a smart, tough competitor. In the 1830s, as New York's population grew, the need for transportation grew. For ten years, Vanderbilt did whatever it took to protect his steamboat company. He was fierce but honest, always finding ways to improve service while still keeping costs down.

Finally, other competitors offered to pay him a great deal of money to buy his company. They paid even more for his promise not to run another steamboat on the Hudson River for ten years!

The Hudson River Route from New York City to Albany

This photo of Vanderbilt was taken in 1845 when he was about fifty years old.

A Millionaire

In 1843, after the sale of his Hudson River company, Vanderbilt started yet another steamship business. This one didn't travel on the Hudson River. Instead, its steamships carried passengers along the coast of the Atlantic Ocean. Vanderbilt's ships sailed from New York to Massachusetts and Rhode Island. His Atlantic coast steamships were among the fastest and most comfortable in the world.

By 1846, Vanderbilt was a millionaire. In those days, it was extremely rare for anyone to have that much money.

Panning for gold in California

The Gold Rush

In 1848, gold was discovered in California. Tens of thousands of Americans traveled west to try to find their fortunes. For most, California was far away. Vanderbilt knew he could make money from the gold rush by providing transportation to the West.

Vanderbilt ran steamships from New York City and New Orleans to California. Other companies did the same, but their ships took much longer because they sailed around the southern tip of South America. Vanderbilt, however, had found a shortcut overland in Central America. He traveled to Nicaragua, leading the journey to set up the new route.

Other businesses knew that competing against Vanderbilt cost a lot of money. Vanderbilt's gold rush competitors offered to buy his company. After a few years, Vanderbilt sold once more—and added to his growing fortune.

Vanderbilt and his competitors helped people get to California. Most of those people didn't find gold but built successful businesses and towns in the new state of California. As result, not only did the transportation companies grow stronger and richer, but so did the United States.

San Francisco's harbor was crowded with boats.

A New Empire Begins

In 1861, the United States was torn apart by the Civil War. At that time, Vanderbilt owned steamboats that crossed the ocean. He let one of his fastest steamboats be used by the North during the war. In the end, he gave the boat to the government. Some say he did so because he was now less interested in steamships than in another form of transportation.

Railroads had been around since about 1830. As a younger man, Vanderbilt hadn't liked them because he didn't think they could make money. He also was almost killed in a railroad accident in 1833. But, by the 1850s, Vanderbilt's thinking had changed. He started investing money in the New York & Harlem Railroad. By 1863, he had invested so much money in the company that he now owned it.

Vanderbilt let this steamship be used by the Union during the Civil War.

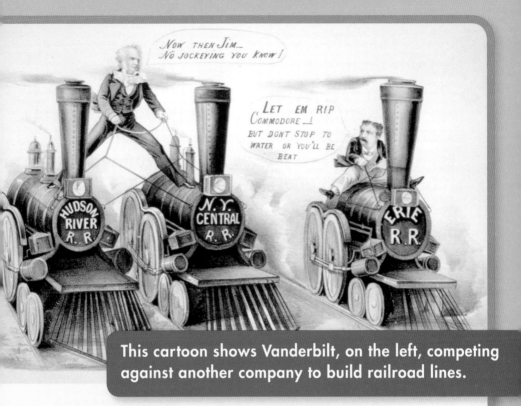

This cartoon shows Vanderbilt, on the left, competing against another company to build railroad lines.

When Vanderbilt bought the New York & Harlem Railroad, it was in bad shape. Under Vanderbilt's ownership, the railroad company greatly improved.

Now Vanderbilt began to build a new railroad empire. At over 70 years old, Vanderbilt still worked and fought hard. As Vanderbilt bought other railroads and combined them, he improved America's railroad system. Older railroad companies had short routes, odd schedules, and bad equipment. Vanderbilt's company had regular schedules and longer routes. The ride was also more comfortable. By 1873, Vanderbilt's rail empire covered the northeastern United States.

Trains from Vanderbilt's many railroad companies would begin or end their routes in New York City. In the late 1860s, Vanderbilt began building Grand Central Terminal in Manhattan. Train lines began or ended at this terminal.

In 1873, hard times hit the American **economy**. Many people lost their jobs, and many businesses closed. But Vanderbilt kept thousands of people working on the terminal. The money they earned and spent kept things from growing even worse.

Grand Central Station

Vanderbilt died in 1877 at the age of 82. He was thought to be the richest man in the country. He was a self-made man who came from a farming family and left behind a fortune of about $100 million.

During Vanderbilt's lifetime, America had changed dramatically. In his young years, the country's main business was agriculture. In his old age, America was filled with new factories and new technologies. Vanderbilt's ships and railroads helped connect different parts of the growing country. They made Vanderbilt a fortune, but they also made the United States a stronger and richer country as well.

Glossary

competitor a company that is in the same type of business as another company

economy the ways a country manages its resources to help people meet their wants and needs

entrepreneur person who takes on the risk of starting a new business

invest to pay money into a business in the hope of making a profit

monopoly the complete control of a type of business

profit money made from a business or investment after expenses are paid

technology the use of scientific knowledge or tools to make or do something